SELECTIONS FROM O BROTHER, WHERE ART THOU?

Artwork and photos courtesy of Touchstone Pictures

Arranged by Jim Schustedt

ISBN 978-0-634-04902-6

HAL•LEONARD® CORPORATION

7777 W. BLUEMOUND RD. P.O. BOX 13819 MILWAUKEE, WI 53213

Visit Hal Leonard Online at
www.halleonard.com

The Big Rock Candy Mountain

Words, Music and Arrangement by Harry K. McClintock

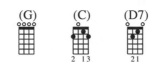

G tuning:
(5th-1st) G–D–G–B–D
Capo V
Key of C

Intro
Moderately

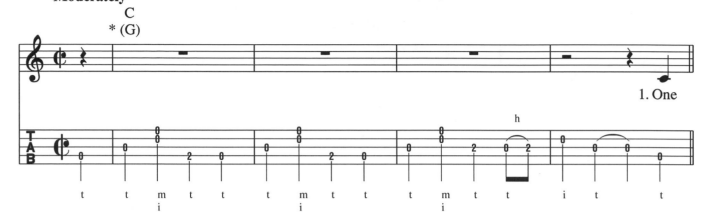

1. One

Verse

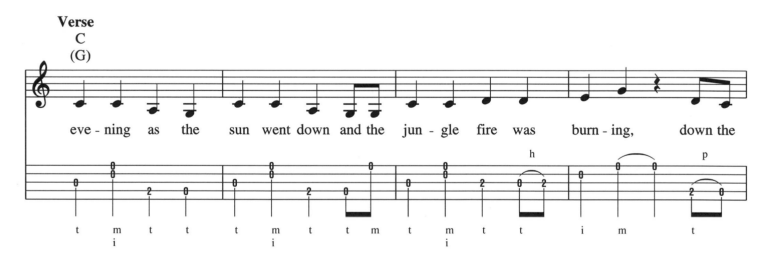

eve- ning as the sun went down and the jun- gle fire was burn- ing, down the

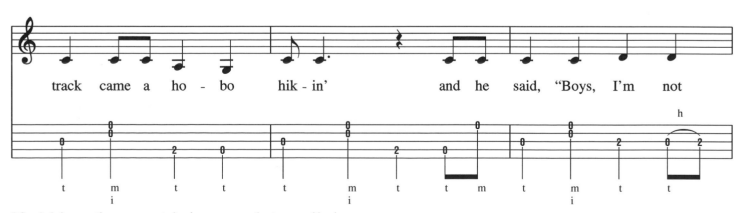

track came a ho- bo hik- in' and he said, "Boys, I'm not

* Symbols in parentheses represent chord names respective to capoed banjo.
  Symbols above reflect actual sounding chords. Capoed fret is "0" in tab.

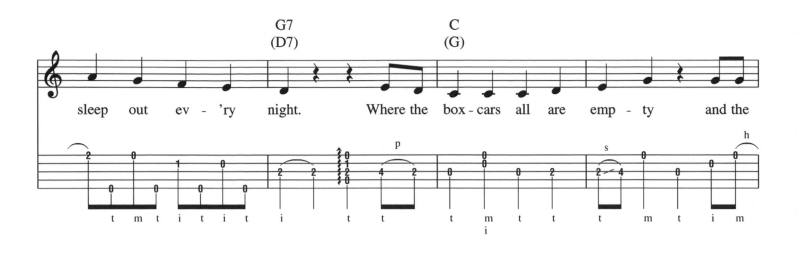

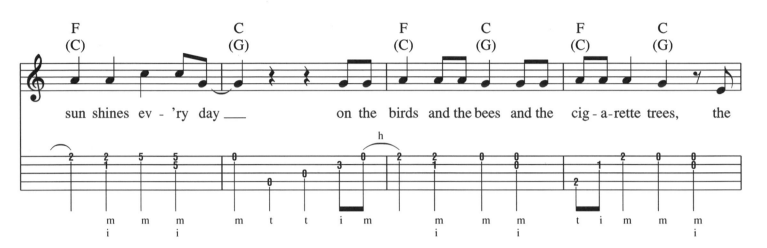

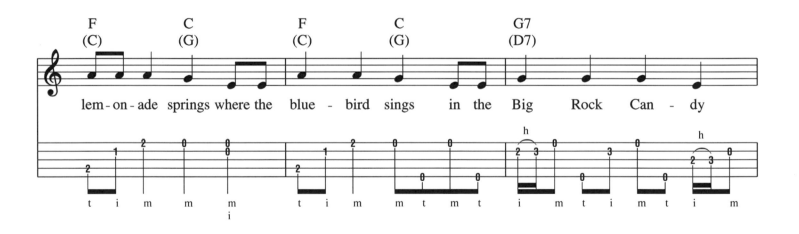

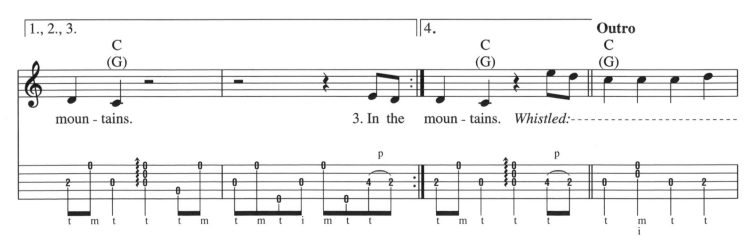

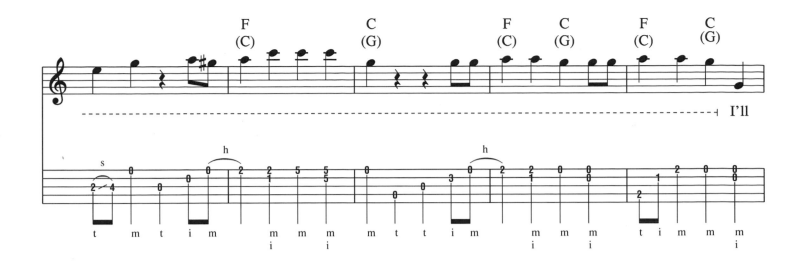

I'll

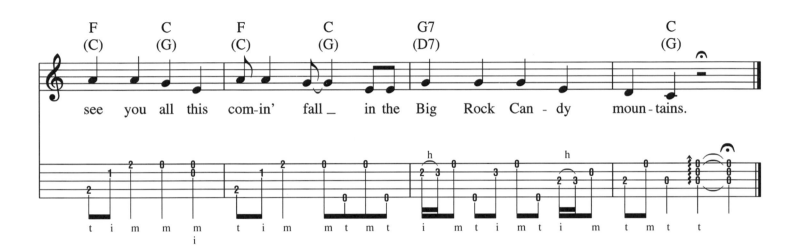

see you all this com-in' fall _ in the Big Rock Can - dy moun-tains.

Additional Lyrics

3. In the Big Rock Candy mountains, all the cops have wooden legs
And the bulldogs all have rubber teeth and the hens lay soft boiled eggs.
The farmers' trees are full of fruit and the barns are full of hay.
Oh, I'm bound to go where there ain't no snow,
Where the rain don't fall, the wind don't blow
In the Big Rock Candy mountains.

4. In the Big Rock Candy mountains, you never change your socks
And the little streams of alcohol come a trickling down the rocks.
The brakeman have to tip their hats and the railroad bulls are blind.
There's a lake of stew and of whiskey too.
You can paddle all around 'em in a big canoe
In the Big Rock Candy mountains.

5. In the Big Rock Candy mountains, the jails are made of tin
And you can walk right out again as soon as you are in.
There ain't no short handled shovels, no axes, saws or picks.
I'm a goin' to stay where you sleep all day,
Where they hung the jerk that invented work,
In the Big Rock Candy mountains.

You Are My Sunshine

Words and Music by Jimmie Davis and Charles Mitchell

G tuning, down 1/2 step:
(5th-1st) Gb–Db–Gb–Bb–Db
Key of G

Intro
Moderately

1. The oth - er night dear, _____ as I lay _ sleep - ing
2., 3., 4. *See additional lyrics*

I dreamed I held you in my arms.

But when I woke, dear, _____ I was mis - tak - en

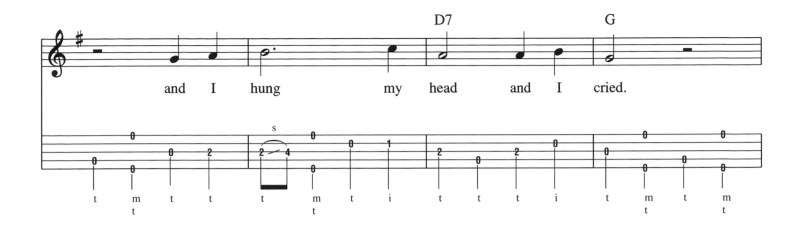

and I hung my head and I cried.

Chorus

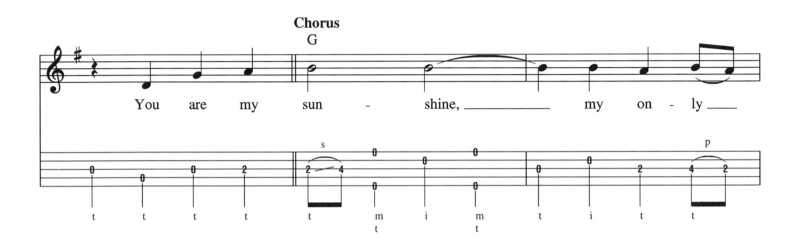

You are my sun - shine, _____ my on - ly _____

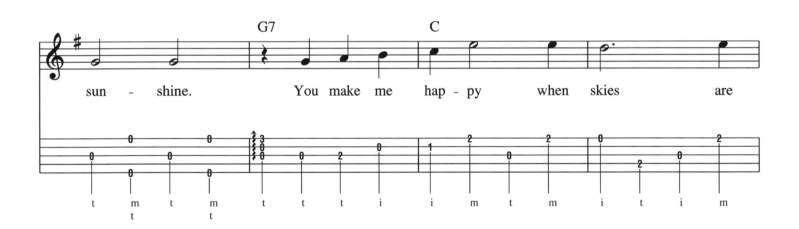

sun - shine. You make me hap - py when skies are

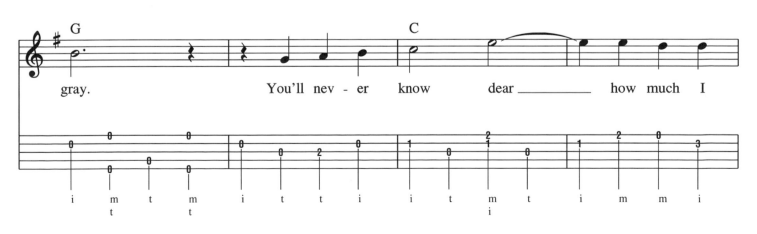

gray. You'll nev - er know dear _____ how much I

love ___ you. Please don't take my sun - shine a -

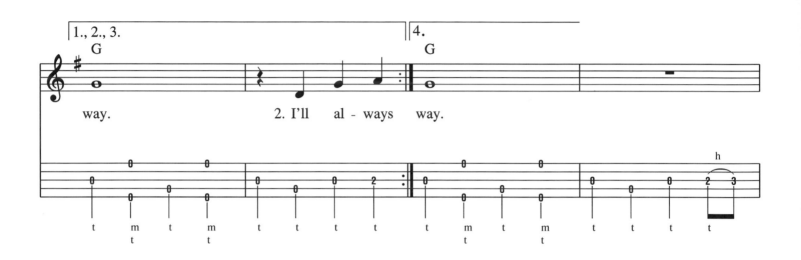

way.   2. I'll al - ways way.

Outro

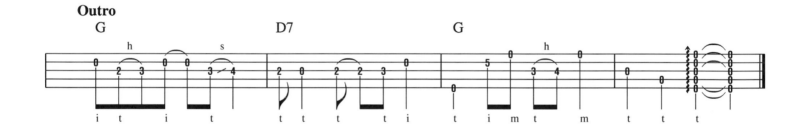

Additional Lyrics

2. I'll always love you and make you happy
   If you will only say the same.
   But if you leave me and love another,
   You'll regret it all some day.

3. You told me once, dear, you really loved me
   And no one could come between.
   But now you've left me to love another.
   You have shattered all of my dreams.

4. In all my dreams, dear, you seem to leave me.
   When I awake my poor heart pains.
   So won't you come back and make me happy.
   I'll forgive, dear, I'll take the blame.

I Am a Man of Constant Sorrow

Words and Music by Carter Stanley

G tuning:
(5th–1st) G–D–G–B–D
Key of G

Moderately

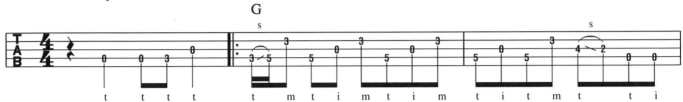

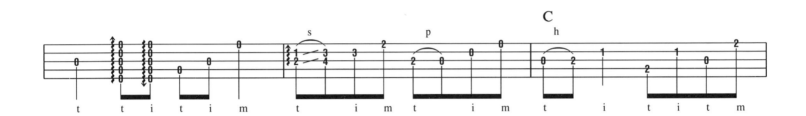

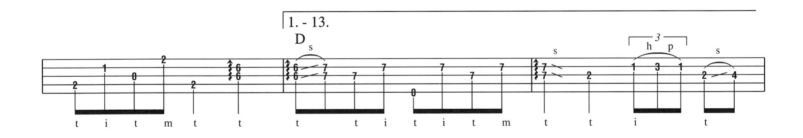

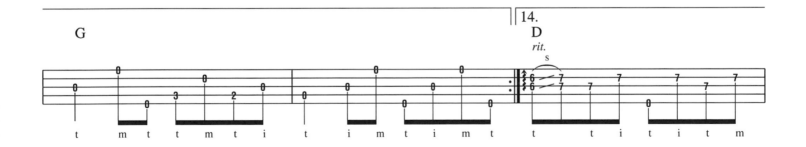

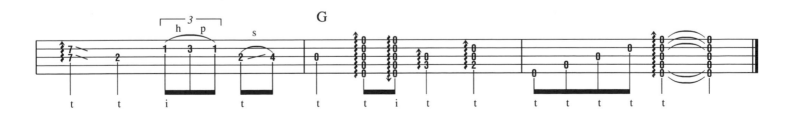

Down to the River to Pray

Traditional

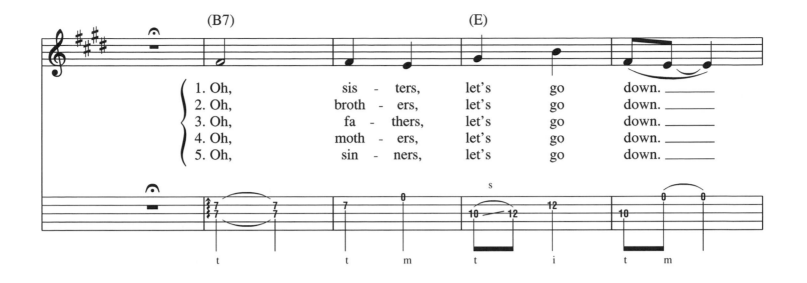

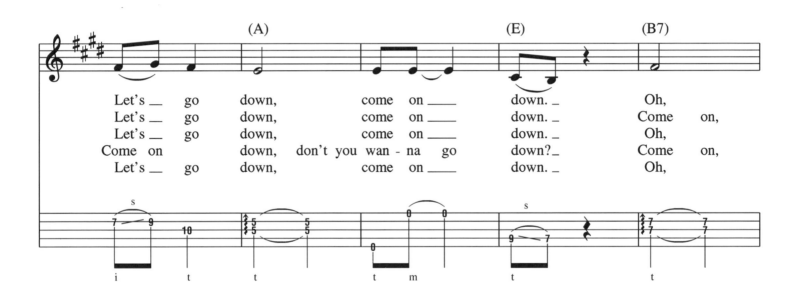

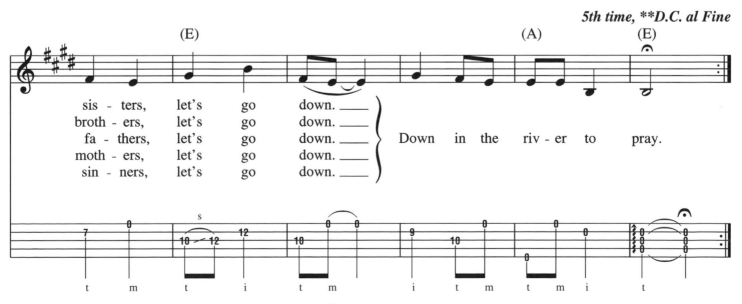

** Repeat back to the beginning of the song and play until the directive *Fine.*

Keep on the Sunny Side

Words and Music by A.P. Carter

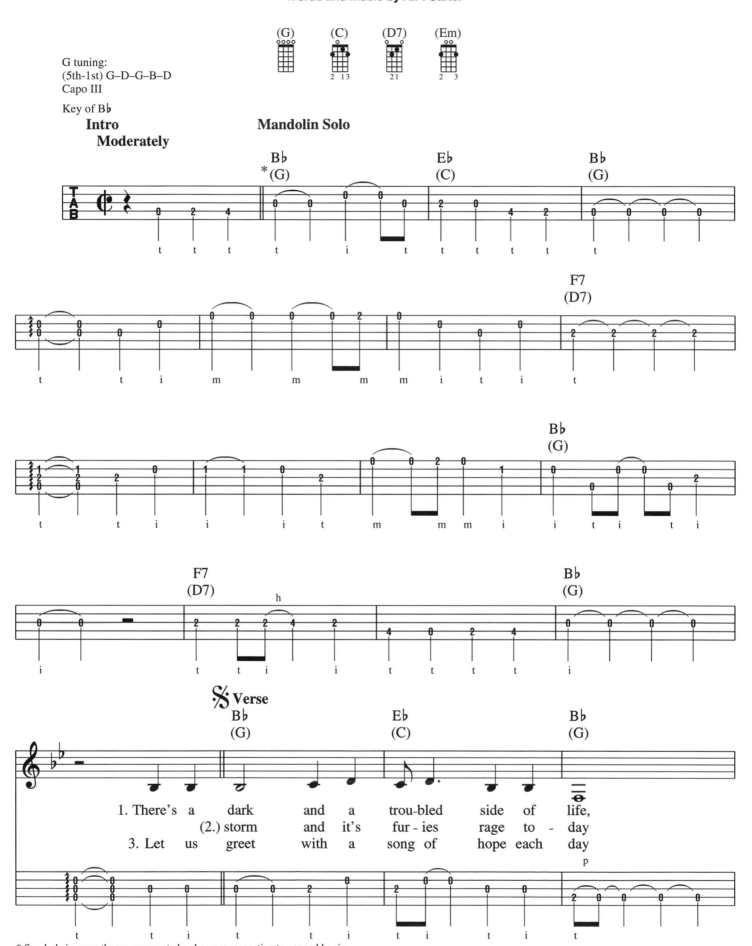

G tuning:
(5th-1st) G–D–G–B–D
Capo III

Key of B♭

Intro
Moderately

Mandolin Solo

1. There's a dark and a trou-bled side of life,
(2.) storm and it's fur-ies rage to-day
3. Let us greet with a song of hope each day

* Symbols in parentheses represent chord names respective to capoed banjo.
  Symbols above reflect actual sounding chords. Capoed fret is "0" in tab.

13

sun-ny side. Keep on the sun-ny side of life.

It will help us ev-'ry day, ___ it will bright-en all the

To Coda 1 $\oplus$ *To Coda 2* $\oplus$

way if we'll keep on the sun-ny side of life.

* *3rd time, D.S.S. al Coda 2*

Dobro Solo

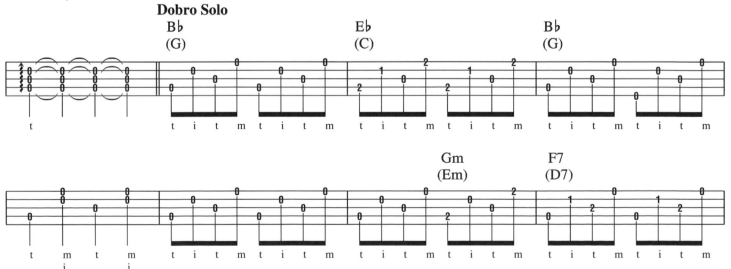

* Go back to the double sign " $\mathcal{S}\mathcal{S}$ " and play until *"To Coda 2,"*
  then skip ahead to the section labeled **"Coda 2."**

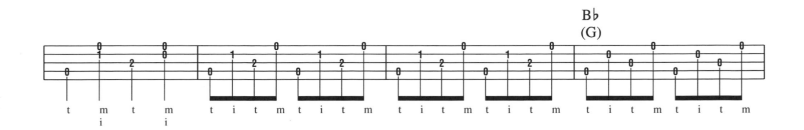

D.S. al Coda 1

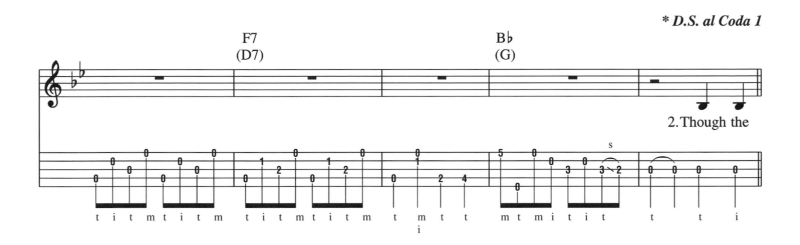

2. Though the

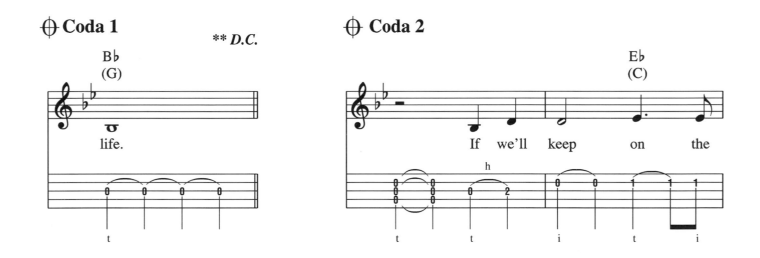

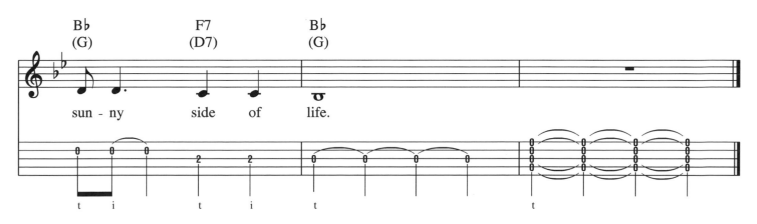

* Go back to the sign "𝄋" and play until *"To Coda 1,"*
   then skip ahead to the section labeled **"Coda 1."**
** Go back to the beginning.

I'll Fly Away

Words and Music by Albert E. Brumley

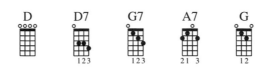

D tuning:
(5th–1st) F#–D–F#–A–D

Key of D

Moderately **Intro/Mandolin Solo**

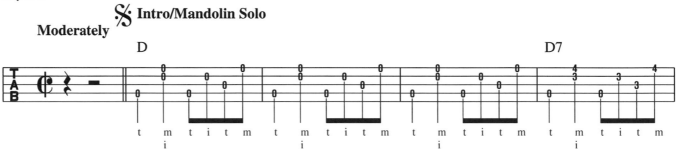

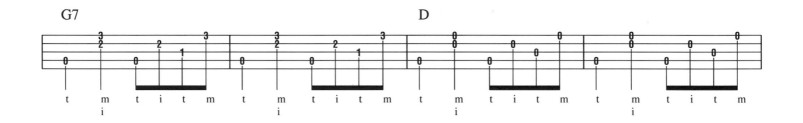

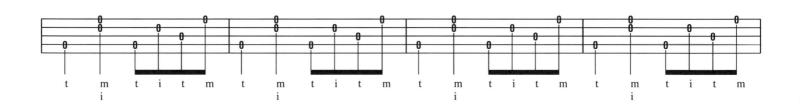

To Coda 1

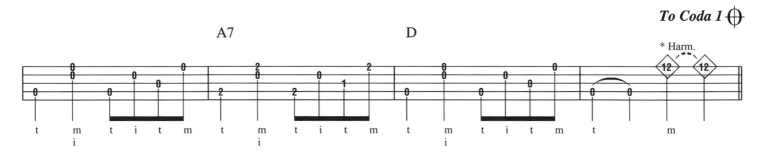

* Harmonics are produced by picking the note while the fret-hand
lightly touches the string directly over the fret indicated.

Chorus

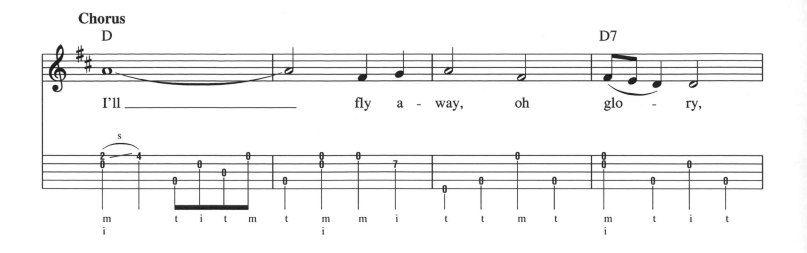

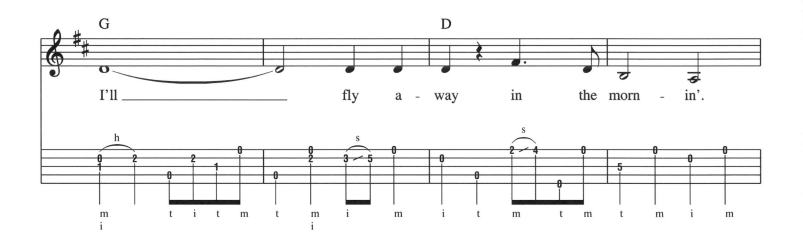

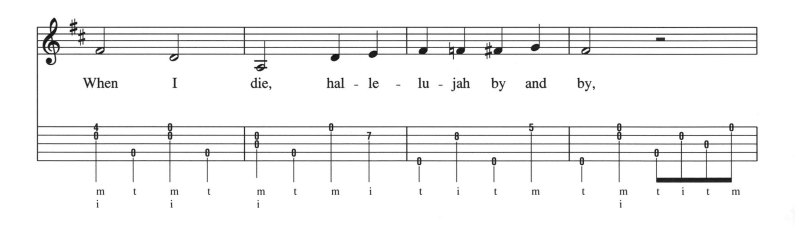

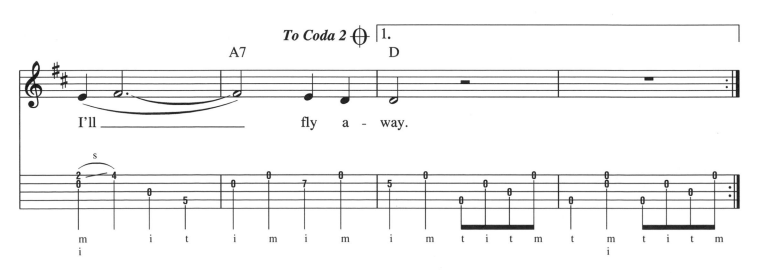

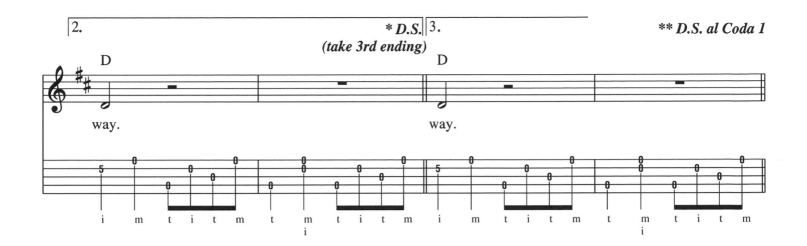

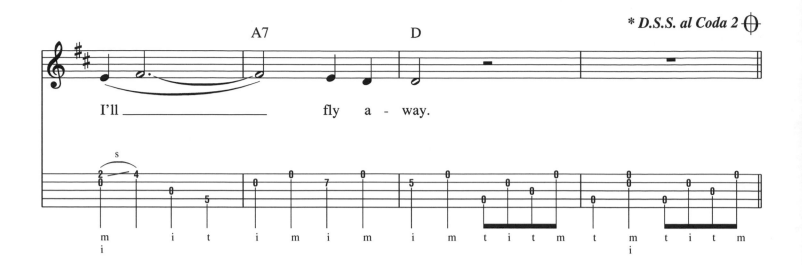

Coda 2
Outro

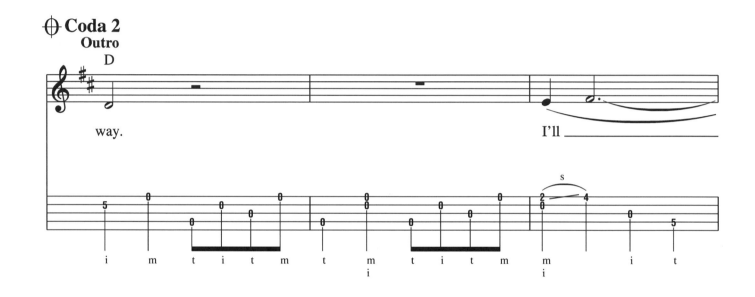

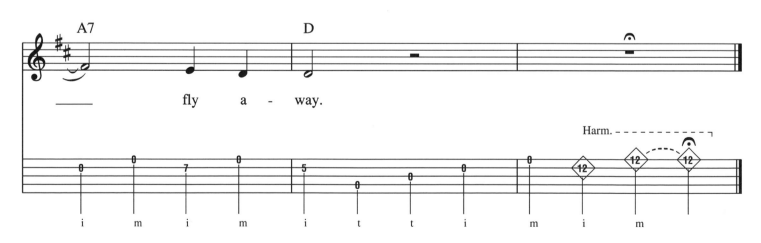

* Go back to the double sign "𝄋 𝄋" and play until *"To Coda 2,"* then skip ahead to the section labeled **"Coda 2."**

In the Highways
(I'll Be Somewhere Working for My Lord)

Words and Music by Maybelle Carter

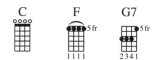

C tuning, up 1/2 step:
(5th-1st) G#–C#–E#–G#–C#

Key of C

Intro
Moderately
N.C.

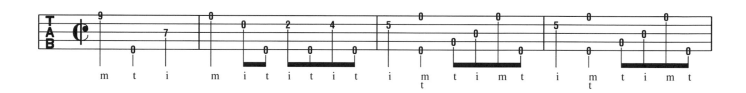

Verse

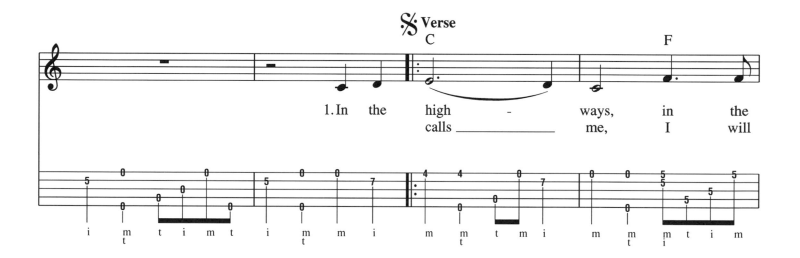

1. In the high - ways, in the
calls _____ me, I will

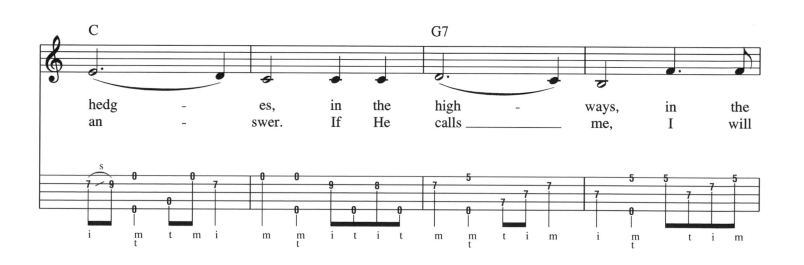

hedg - es, in the high - ways, in the
an - swer. If He calls _____ me, I will

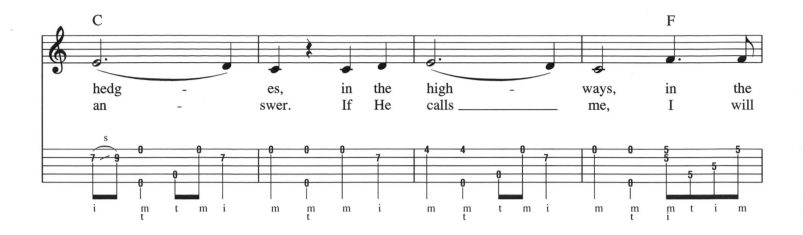

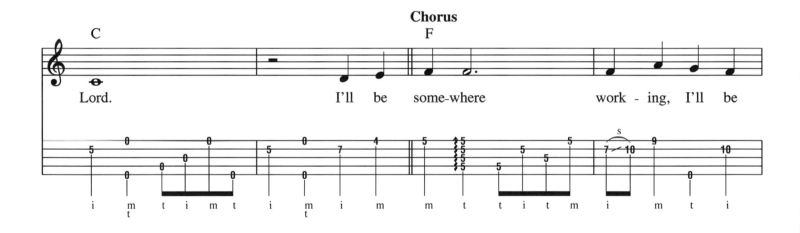

Lord. _____ I'll be some-where work-ing, I'll be

some - where work - ing, I'll be some-where a work - ing for my

*2nd time, D.S. al Coda
(take 1st lyrics)*

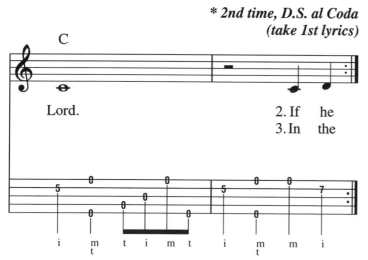

Lord.

2. If he
3. In the

⊕ **Coda**

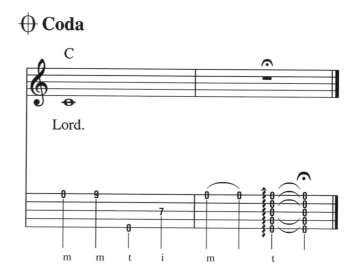

Lord.

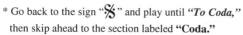
* Go back to the sign "𝄋" and play until *"To Coda,"*
then skip ahead to the section labeled **"Coda."**

Didn't Leave Nobody but the Baby

Words and Music by Gillian Welch, T-Bone Burnett, Alan Lomax and Mrs. Sidney Carter

Tuning:
(5th-1st) B♭–D–G–B–D
Capo III

Key of B♭

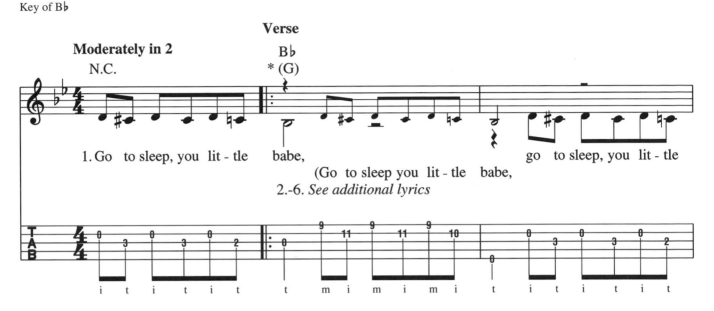

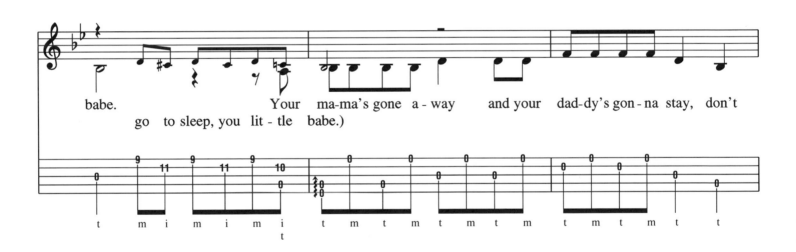

* Symbol in parenthesis represents chord name respective to capoed banjo.
  Symbol above reflects actual sounding chord. Capoed fret is "0" in tab.

2. Go to sleep, you little babe,
    (Go to sleep, you little babe.)
    Go to sleep, you little babe,
    (Go to sleep, you little babe.)
    Everybody's gone in the cotton and the corn,
    Didn't leave nobody but the baby.

3. You're sweet, little babe,
    (You're sweet, little babe.)
    You're sweet, little babe,
    (You're sweet, little babe.)
    Honey in the rock and the sugar don't stop.
    Gonna bring a bottle to the baby.

4. Don't you weep, pretty babe,
    (Don't you weep, pretty babe.)
    Don't you weep, pretty babe,
    (Don't you weep, pretty babe.)
    She's long gone with her red shoes on,
    Gonna need another lovin' baby.

5. Go to sleep, little babe,
    (Go to sleep, little babe.)
    Go to sleep, little babe,
    (Go to sleep, little babe.)
    You and me and the devil makes three,
    Don't need no other lovin' baby.

6. Go to sleep, you little babe,
    (Go to sleep, little babe.)
    Go to sleep, little babe,
    (Go to sleep, little babe.)
    Come lay your bones on the alabster stones
    And be my ever-lovin' baby.

I Am Weary (Let Me Rest)

Words and Music by Pete (Roberts) Kuykendall

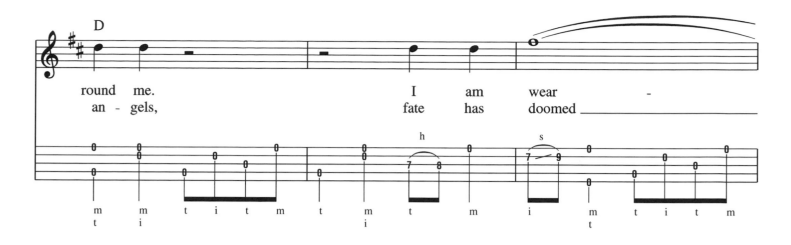

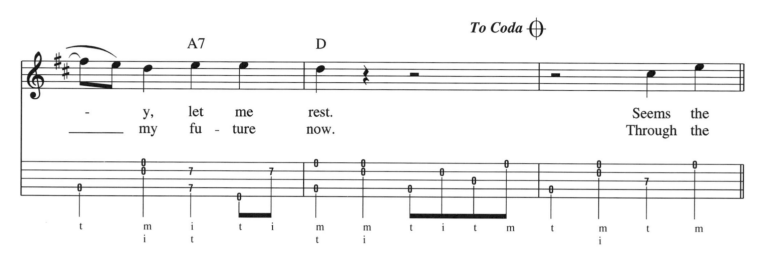

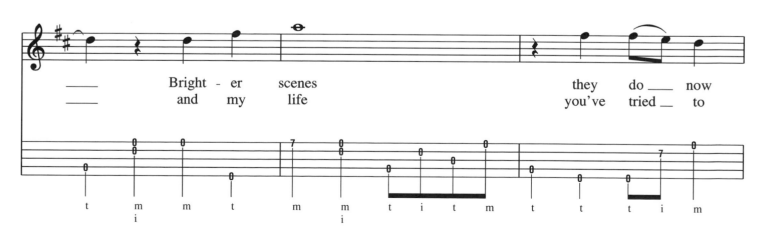

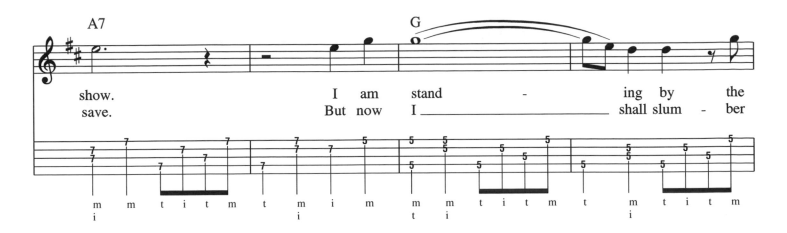

show.
save.

I am stand - - - ing by the
But now I _____ shall slum - ber

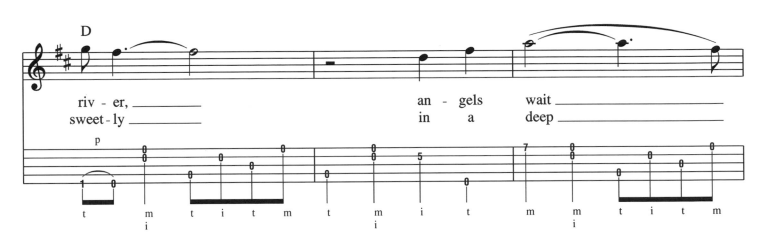

riv - er, _____
sweet - ly _____

an - gels wait _____
in a deep _____

*2nd time, D.S. al Coda
(take 1st lyrics)

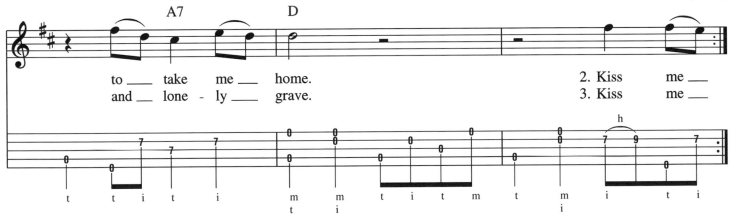

to ___ take me ___ home.
and ___ lone - ly ___ grave.

2. Kiss me ___
3. Kiss me ___

⊕ Coda

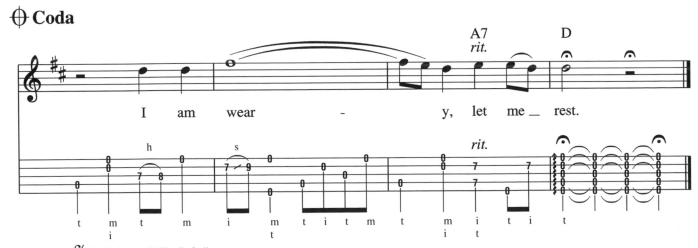

I am wear - - - y, let me ___ rest.

* Go back to the sign "𝄋" and play until *"To Coda,"*
then skip ahead to the section labeled **"Coda."**

In the Jailhouse Now

Words and Music by Jimmie Rodgers

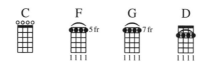

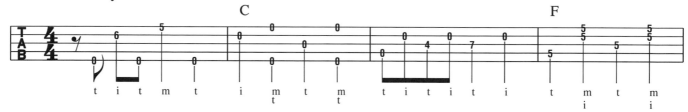

C tuning, down 1/2 step:
(5th-1st) F#–B–F#–B–D#

Key of C

Intro
Moderately

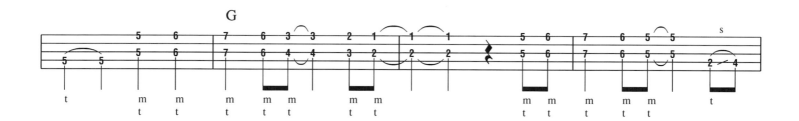

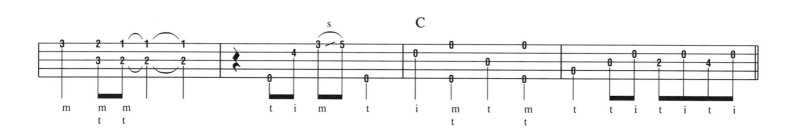

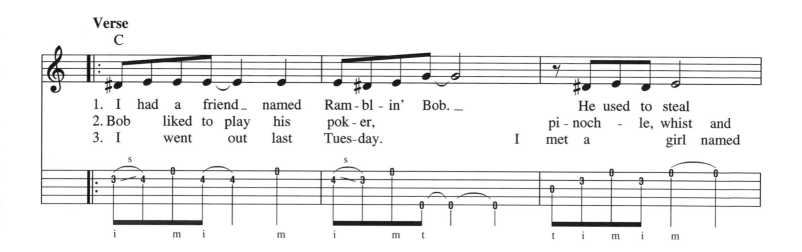

Verse

1. I had a friend named Ram-bl-in' Bob. He used to steal
2. Bob liked to play his pok-er, pi-noch-le, whist and
3. I went out last Tues-day. I met a girl named

gam - ble and rob. ___ He thought he was ___ the smart - est guy ___ a -
eu - chre, but shoot - in' dice ___ was his fav - 'rite
Su - sie. I said I was ___ the swell - est guy ___ a -

F

round. Well, I found out last
game. Well, he got throwed in
round. Well, we start - ed to spend - in' my

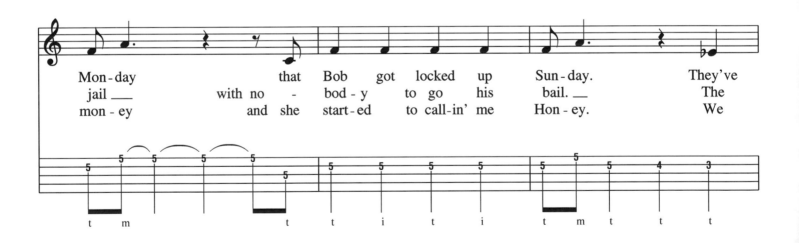

Mon - day that Bob got locked up Sun - day. They've
jail ___ with no - bod - y to go his bail. ___ The
mon - ey and she start - ed to call - in' me Hon - ey. We

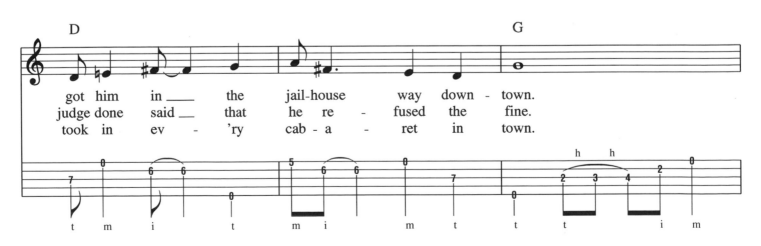

D   G

got him in ___ the jail - house way down - town.
judge done said ___ that he re - fused the fine.
took in ev - 'ry cab - a - ret in town.

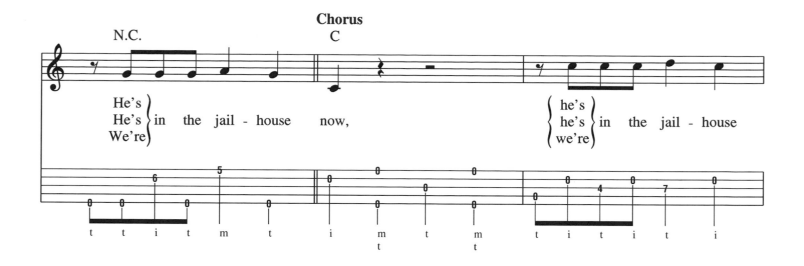

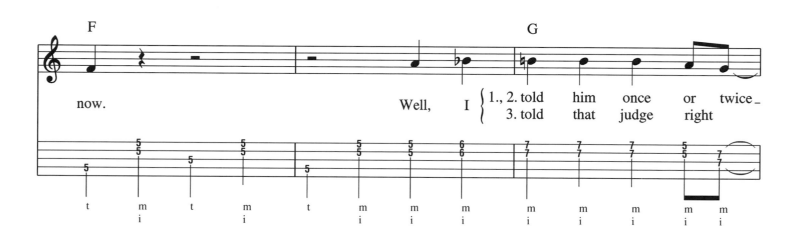

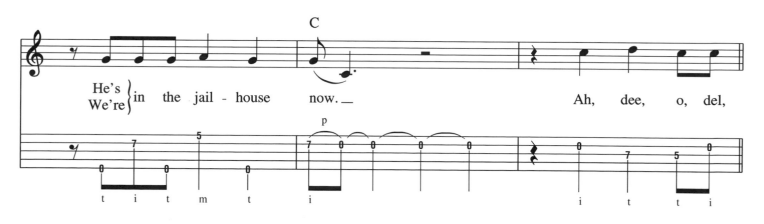

Interlude

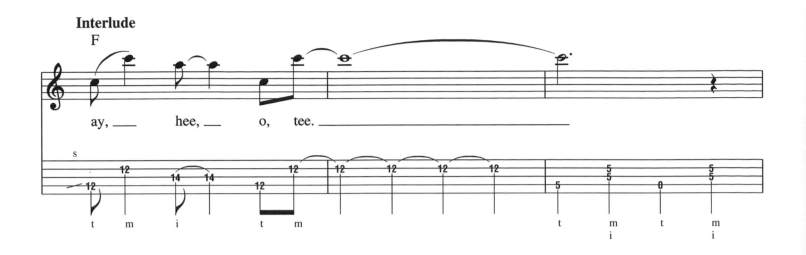

ay, ___ hee, ___ o, tee. _____

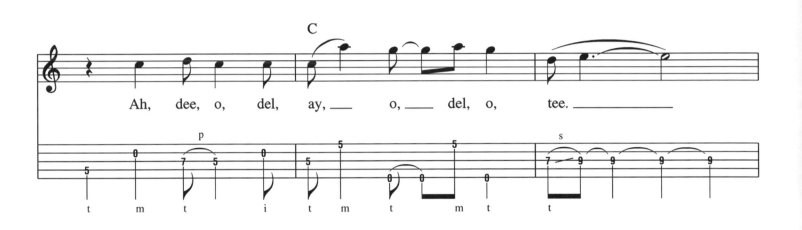

Ah, dee, o, del, ay, ___ o, ___ del, o, tee. _____

Yo, del, ay, hee, hee, ___ yo, del, ay, hee, hee, ___ yo, del,

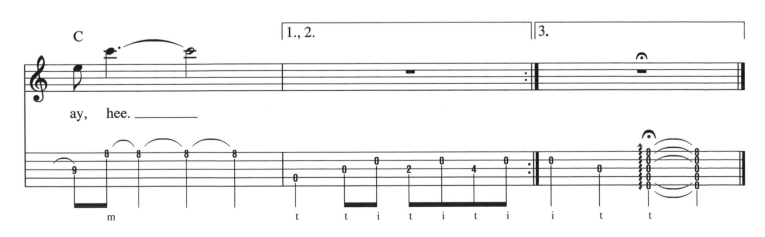

ay, hee. _____

I Am a Man of Constant Sorrow

Words and Music by Carter Stanley

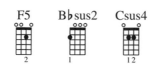

Fsus4 tuning:
(5th–1st) F–C–F–B♭–C

Key of F

Intro

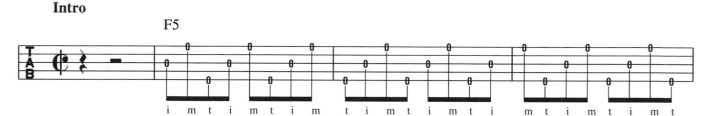

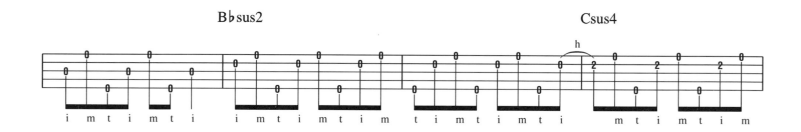

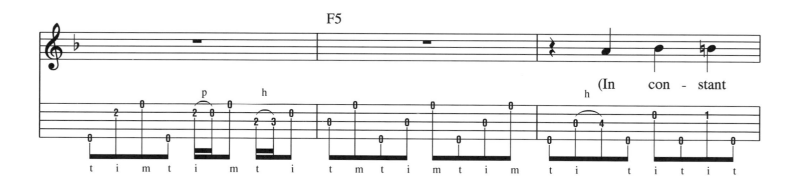

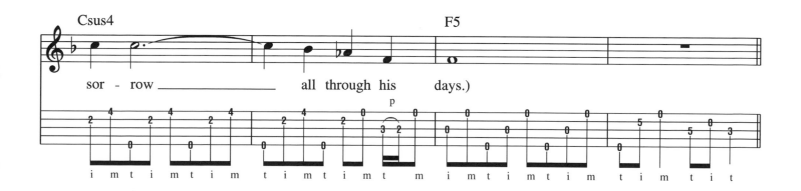

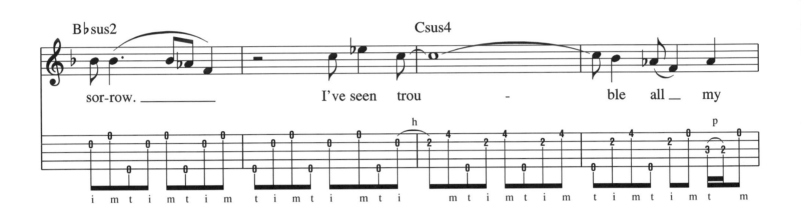

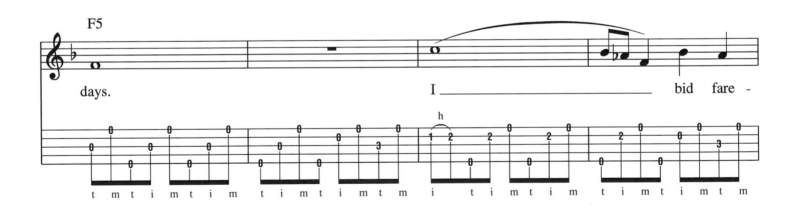

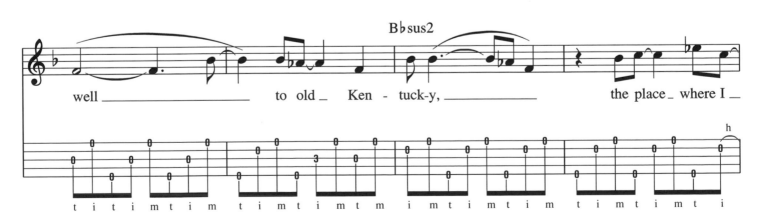

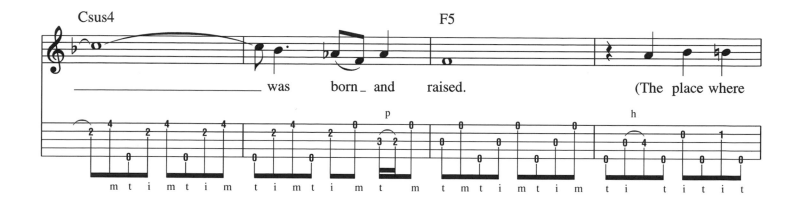

was born_ and raised.   (The place where

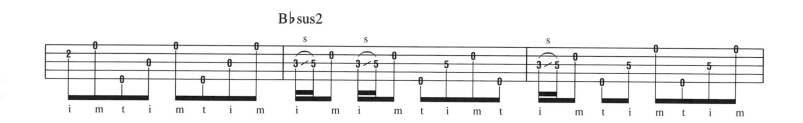

To Coda ⊕

he _____ was born and raised.)

Banjo Solo

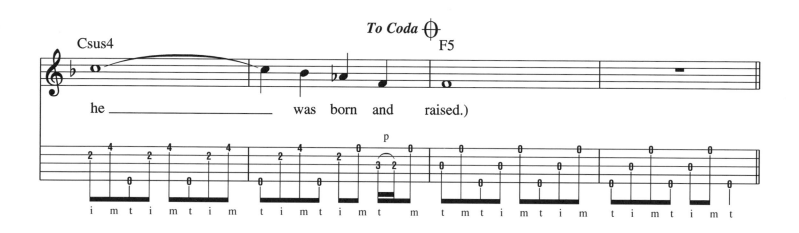

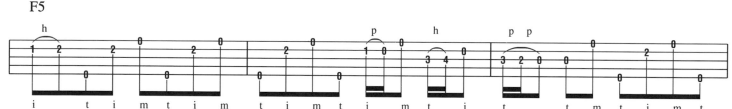

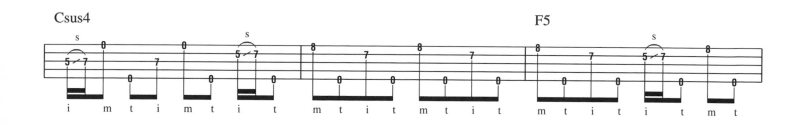

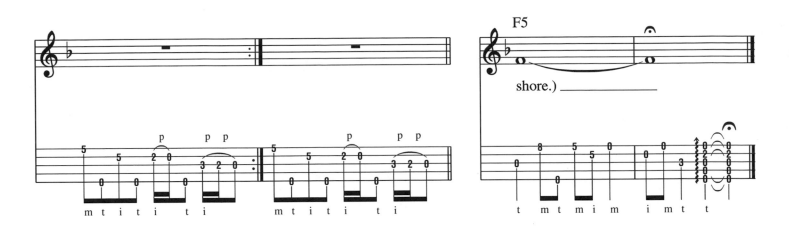

Additional Lyrics

2. For six long years I've been in trouble,
   No pleasure here on earth I've found.
   For in this world I'm bound to ramble.
   I have no friends to help me now.
   (He has no friends to help him now.)

3. It's fare thee well, my own true lover.
   I never expect to see you again.
   For I'm bound to ride that northern railroad.
   Perhaps I'll die upon that train.
   (Perhaps he'll die upon this train.)

4. You can bury me in sunny valley
   For many years where I may lay.
   Pray and you may learn to love another
   While I am sleeping in my grave.
   (While he is sleeping in his grave.)

5. Maybe your friends think I'm just a stranger,
   My face you never will see no more.
   But there is one promise that is given,
   I'll meet you on God's golden shore.
   (He'll meet you on God's golden shore.)

* Go back to the sign "𝄋" and play until *"To Coda,"*
then skip ahead to the section labeled **"Coda."**

Angel Band

Words and Music by Ralph Stanley

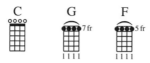

C tuning, down 1/2 step:
(5th-1st) F#–B–F#–B–D#

Key of C

Intro
Moderately

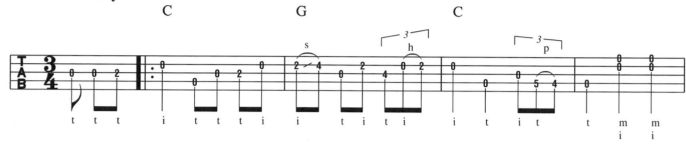

Verse

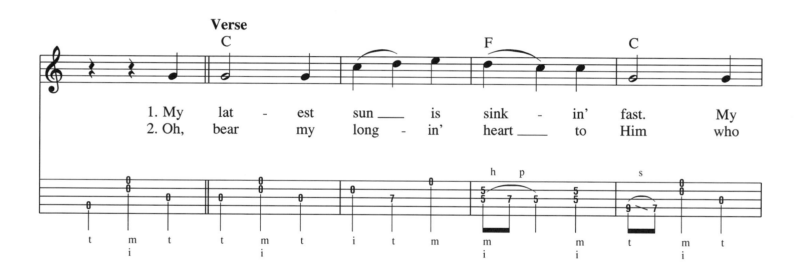

1. My lat - est sun ___ is sink - in' fast. My
2. Oh, bear my long - in' heart ___ to Him who

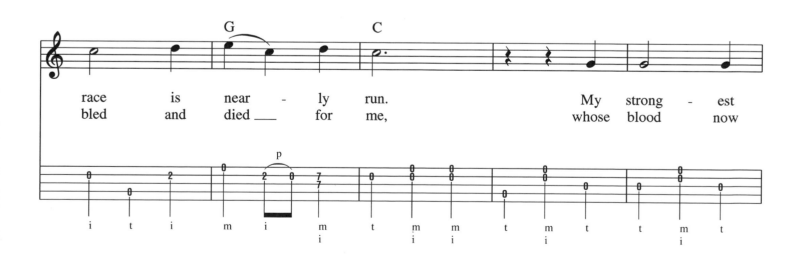

race is near - ly run. My strong - est
bled and died ___ for me, whose blood now

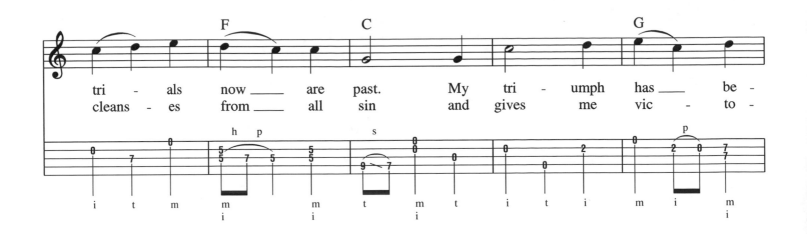

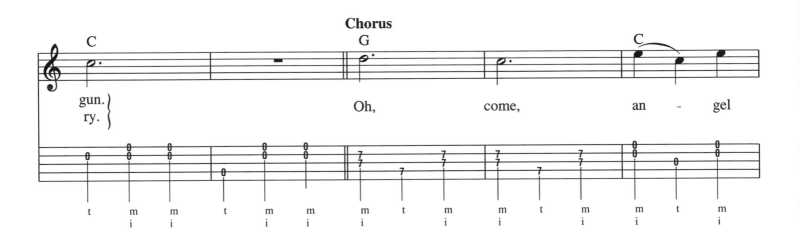

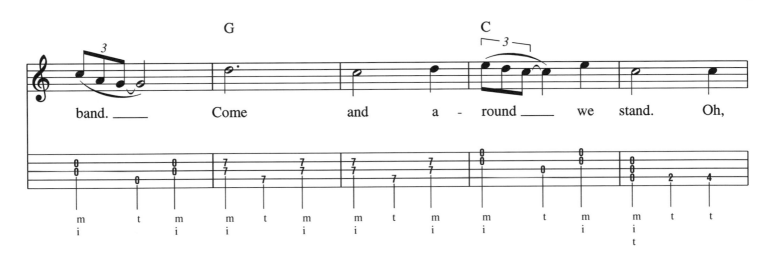

mor - tal home. _____ Oh, bear me a - way on your

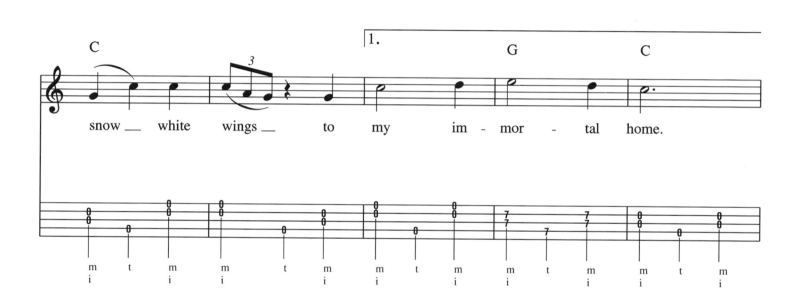

snow _ white wings _ to my im - mor - tal home.

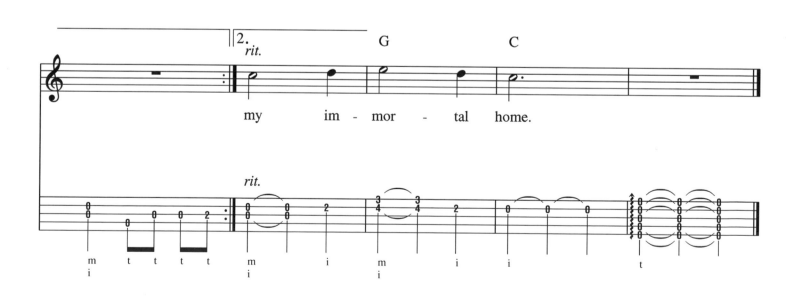

my im - mor - tal home.

Banjo Notation Legend

TABLATURE graphically represents the banjo fingerboard. Each horizontal line represents a string, and each number represents a fret.

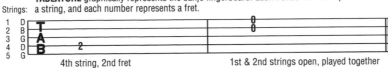

4th string, 2nd fret   1st & 2nd strings open, played together

TIME SIGNATURE:
The upper number indicates the number of beats per measure, the lower number indicates that a quarter note gets one beat.

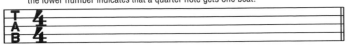

CUT TIME:
Each note's time value should be cut in half. As a result, the music will be played twice as fast as it is written.

QUARTER NOTE:
time value = 1 beat

EIGHTH NOTES:
time value = 1/2 beat each

single   in series

SIXTEENTH NOTES:
time value = 1/4 beat each

single   in series

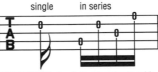

DOTTED QUARTER NOTE:
time value = 1 1/2 beat

TIE: Pick the 1st note only, then let it sustain for the combined time value.

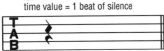

TRIPLET: Three notes played in the same time normally occupied by two notes of the same time value.

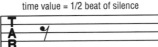

GRACE NOTE: A quickly played note with no time value of its own. The grace note and the note following it only occupy the time value of the second note.

RITARD: A gradual slowing of the tempo or speed of the song.

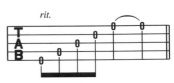

QUARTER REST:
time value = 1 beat of silence

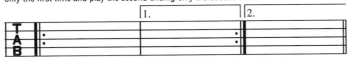

EIGHTH REST:
time value = 1/2 beat of silence

HALF REST:
time value = 2 beats of silence

WHOLE REST:
time value = 4 beats of silence

ENDINGS: When a repeated section has a first and second ending, play the first ending only the first time and play the second ending only the second time.

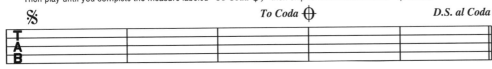

REPEAT SIGNS: Play the music between the repeat signs two times.

D.S. AL CODA:
Play through the music until you complete the measure labeled *"D.S. al Coda,"* then go back to the sign (𝄋).
Then play until you complete the measure labeled *"To Coda ⊕,"* then skip to the section labeled *"⊕ Coda."*

𝄋   *To Coda* ⊕   *D.S. al Coda*   ⊕ *Coda*

HAMMER-ON: Strike the first (lower) note with one finger, then sound the higher note (on the same string) with another finger by fretting it without picking.

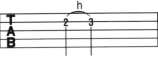

PULL-OFF: Place both fingers on the notes to be sounded. Strike the first note and without picking, pull the finger off to sound the second (lower) note.

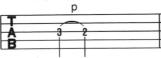

SLIDE UP: Strike the first note and then slide the same fret-hand finger up to the second note. The second note is not struck.

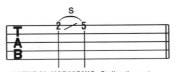

SLIDE DOWN: Strike the first note and then slide the same fret-hand finger down to the second note. The second note is not struck.

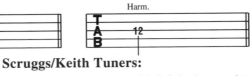

HALF-STEP CHOKE: Strike the note and bend the string up 1/2 step.

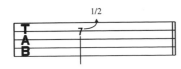

WHOLE-STEP CHOKE: Strike the note and bend the string up one step.

NATURAL HARMONIC: Strike the note while the fret-hand lightly touches the string directly over the fret indicated.

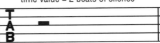

BRUSH: Play the notes of the chord indicated by quickly rolling them from bottom to top.

Scruggs/Keith Tuners:

HALF-TWIST UP: Strike the note, twist tuner up 1/2 step, and continue playing.

HALF-TWIST DOWN: Strike the note, twist tuner down 1/2 step, and continue playing.

WHOLE-TWIST UP: Strike the note, twist tuner up one step, and continue playing.

Right Hand Fingerings

t = thumb   i = index finger   m = middle finger